Labyrinth Of Flowers

a collection of honest thoughts

Radeyah Roni

BookLeaf
Publishing

India | USA | UK

Made with ❤ on the BookLeaf Publishing Platform
www.bookleafpub.in
www.bookleafpub.com

Dedication

to my amazing family, who has given me more than i
could ever imagine, i love you guys so very much

Preface

As a young Bengali Muslim woman, I carry the rich traditions and resilient spirit of my heritage close to my heart. My upbringing has gifted me with a deep gratitude for the simple joys of life. Yet I am also acutely aware of the harsh realities that so many in this world face - injustice, hatred, and suffering.

From a young age, I've felt a calling to use my voice and efforts to uplift others and create positive change. This collection of poetry and stories represents my humble attempt to weave together the vibrant threads of my experiences with an urgent call to embrace compassion and find beauty even in our darkest moments.

May these pages fill you with appreciation for life's simple beauties while stirring your soul to join the vital work of crafting a kinder, more just world for all, and finding resonance with the experiences I've poured into these words.

Acknowledgements

infinite gratitude to my little sister for critiquing every
word that i wrote

a deep thank you to Arushi, my publishing manager, for
guiding me through this thrilling process

when will i rise?

through the storms and shadows, my spirit flows,
when will i rise, where the morning glows?
in whispers of twilight, dreams take flight,
when will i rise, to greet the light?
with hope as my compass, and dreams set high,
when will i rise, to touch the sky?

cloudy moonlight

wispy clouds veil the night sky's face,
obscuring the moon's gentle grace.
cloudy moonlight casts a hushed glow,
bathing the earth in a soft, ethereal flow.

nature's heart

in the heart of nature, blossoms unfold
in the heart of nature, beauty never fades
in the heart of nature, stories are told
in the heart of nature, joy finds its way
with every new season, and every new day

wandering star

my shooting star, time takes its ease,
no need to hurry, just feel the breeze
perhaps we are wanderers, always yearning,
for dreams adrift, forever turning,
shooting stars lost in the night
seeking dreams, a distant light

pinning grace

draped in modesty's gentle embrace,
the fabric frames her radiant face.
not bound by dull pins of conformity's chains,
but graced by a beauty that forever reigns.

the cloth's soft folds, a sacred adornment,
not a restriction but a soul's true ornament.
pinning back whispers that seek to confine,
unveiling a spirit that forever will shine.

no dull pins can tarnish her vibrant heart,
for in modesty's folds, she's set apart.
pinning down stereotypes that aim to diminish,
her grace and her strength will forever flourish.

with every gentle sweep of the fabric's caress,
she pins up misconceptions, letting truth progress.
not weighed down by the dull pins of society's demands,
but uplifted in faith, grace ever at hand.

stop for the view

the meadows are blooming in pastels,
birds singing melodies you've been missing before.
the sky's painted canvas, a masterpiece,
has been there all along, hidden from your sight.
life's grandest delights are the simple things,
they whisper their beauty while our busy mind sings.

an alarm for gratitude

in the shadow of conflict, where darkness abides,
the children who live in hardship hold hope in their eyes.
their spirits remain unbowed, their light never lost.

as we count our blessings, secure in our peace,
let our hearts overflow with gratitude's increase.
for the trials they face, the struggles they brave,
teach us to treasure each moment we save.

their laughter, though muted by the sounds of strife,
reminds us to savor the sweetness of life.
their resilience, forged in the crucible of pain,
inspires us to rise, our own burdens to wane.

so let us give thanks for the gifts we hold dear,
and send our prayers to those living in fear.

orion

the hunter's belts blazes bright, bold in cosmic dreams,
three stars aligned in a perfect trance, illuminating
ancient celestial light.
bow drawn back, arrow already loosed
fate's whisper carried on silken winds, aim true, doubts
reduced.
orion's story, spun in the stars, a destiny written, never
undone.

anchor

in the turbulent seas of life's swell,
where waves of doubt and fear often dwell,
our parents stand, anchors steadfast,
fasten us to a love unsurpassed.
a ballast against the raging tides,
their wisdom ever our compass guides.

shattered reflection

fragments of a soul, scattered and torn,
each piece tells a story, a glimpse into what was.
in the broken pieces, truth is lost, a mosaic of lies.

hell in heaven

envy is hell in heaven's guide,
poisoning bliss with greedy eyes.
admiring beauty, craving what's not yours, hunger's
curse.
lush gardens withering to dust,
as plenty's never quite enough.

one window

one window is all i need,
to see the sacrifies the people around me committed.
to understand the struggle of them, wish them healing
and peace for the complications.
to show them i'm grateful from the depths of my heart
and soul.

some things can't be fixed

a reminder of the past, things we will never know.
in the cracks and crevices, memories reside, stories
without an end.
stiched seams may hold, but scars will always show.

ethereal embrace

an ethereal embrace, tender and true,
a love transcending the cosmos anew.

galaxies apart, yet always near,
together we wander life's course,
walking through shadows, calming all fears.

an unspoken language, our hearts align,
in each other's presence, we find solace,
this sisterly bond, eternal solace.

the sea eventually comes to an end

the waves that thrash and rage today will someday calm
their wilderness.
just as the tides must rage and turn, so too this pain will
cease to burn.
all storms no matter how they frayed, are destined to
fade.

red lipstick

with a mind sharp as damascus steel,
ideas and insights, so profound, so real.
she speaks with wisdom, intellect blazing bright,
yet all they see is her lipstick's red light.

for in their eyes, no matter what heights she scales,
her value's defined by cosmetic details.
her mind revolutionary, yet ignored at a glance,
overshadowed by focus on that lipstick's trance.

anatomy

beneath the skin, we're one and same,
sharing this human, earthly frame.
diverse yet bound by kindred ties.

beyond all superficial traits,
within each soul, truth awaits:
we laugh, we cry, we hope, we fear -
inheritors of joys and tears.

my closure

forgiveness flows, a one-way stream, from my heart to
yours.
though you may never reciprocate, i'll free myself from
bitter weight.

my pardon is what i dictate.
for me, not you, this gift is meant - to release all
resentment's rent.

i forgive you for making me feel weak.
i forgive you for making me feel as if i did not exist.
and i pray your heart may find peace and rest.

handcrafted artistry

with hands so kind, generation's love in every meal,
a gentle touch, a graceful way, in each dish, their hearts
convey.
traditions flow, from one to the next, their love continues
to grow.
though tired, they always care through endless love.

with every bite, a legacy of love and care.

masquerade

in this grand theater of life's design,
we all don masks upon the line.
our truths to disguise,
hiding behind the veil of lies.
yet, in the silence of our souls,
the truth remains, its heavy tolls.
behind the facades we adorn,
lies a truth, forever torn.

honey never expires

a golden elixir, nature's timeless sweet,
a testament of time, stories of the past and future
intertwine.
it hold its grace in its sweet embrace.
with every drop, hope is savored.

www.ingramcontent.com/pod-product-compliance
Lightning Source LLC
Chambersburg PA
CBHW071246140726
47996CB00007B/2783